گول! آٸوکھیلیں!

Goal! Let's Play!

Joe Marriott
Illustrated by Algy Craig Hall

Urdu translation by Qamar Zamani

Mantra Lingua

میں چین ہوں اور
میں روزانہ فٹ بال کھیلتا ہوں۔

I'm Chen and I play
football every day.

Thwack   boing

Goal!

Let's score!

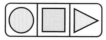

میرا نام ڈےنیلہ ہے۔ مجھے اپنے دوستوں کے ساتھ
باسکٹ بال کھیلنا بہت پسند ہے۔

My name's Daniella.
I love playing basketball
with my friends.

Boing phwoop

through the hoop!

Let's shoot!

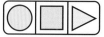

میں چیٹ ہوں اور مجھے اپنی ٹیم کے ساتھ
بیس بال کھیلنے میں بہت مزہ آتا ہے۔

I'm Chet and I love playing
baseball with my team.

WHACK WHIZ

LET'S CATCH!

THUNK ○ **CAUGHT!**

میرا نام فارس ہے۔ ابّا اور میں ایک اونٹ

پر بیٹھے دوڑ لگا رہے ہیں۔

My name's Faris. Daddy and I
are racing on a camel.

Humpety!

Bumpety!

Thumpety!

Let's ride!

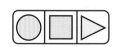

میں کیٹی ہوں اور میں پہاڑی کی چوٹی
پر پتنگ اُڑاتی ہوں۔

I'm Katy and I fly my kite
at the top of the hill.

Let's fly!

Whoosh!

zoom!

Zip!

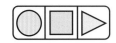

میرا نام پی ایئر ہے۔ میں اپنی کلاس کا سب
سے تیز دوڑنے والا ہوں۔

My name's Pierre. I'm the
fastest runner in my class.

Huff puff whiz whistle!

Let's race!

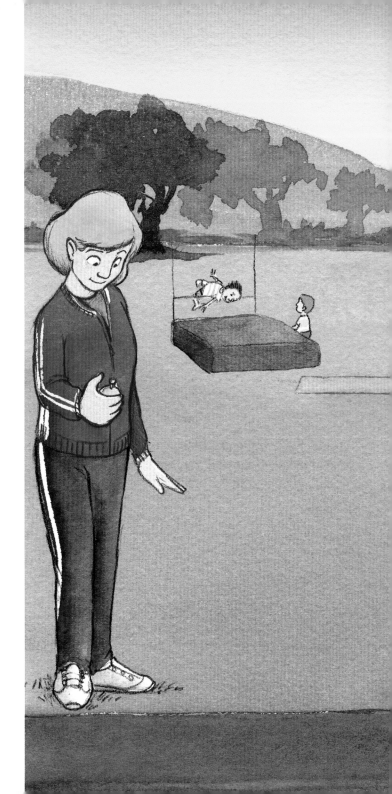

میں نادیہ ہوں اور مجھے اپنی دوستوں کے ساتھ
ٹھنڈے پانی میں تیرنا بہت پسند ہے۔

I'm Nadia and I love swimming
with my friends in the cool water.

splish

splash

sploosh!

Let's dive!

میرا نام جیمس ہے۔ میں ہر سینیچر کی صبح کو اپنے خاندان کے ساتھ ٹینس کھیلتا ہوں۔

My name's James. I play tennis with my family every weekend.

Whack!

Wham!

Boing!

SLAM!

Let's serve!

میں مارتا ہوں اور میں ورزش کے کمرے میں جُوڈو کی مشق کر رہی ہوں۔

I'm Marta and I'm learning judo in the gym.

Spin!

Chop!

Flip!

Flop!

Let's throw!

میں ٹامس ہوں اور
میں برف رانی کر سکتا ہوں۔

I'm Tomas and I can
ski really fast.

Swish! Swerve!

Whiiiiiiiiiiiiizzzzzzzzz z z z!

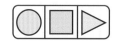

Let's ski!

میرا نام نیتیش ہے۔ مجھے اپنے خاندان
کے ساتھ کرکٹ کھیلنا بے حد پسند ہے۔

My name's Nitesh. I love playing
cricket with my friends and family.

Whooooosh!

Thwaaacc c c ckk!

Let's bowl!

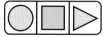